Introduction

I first came across the Leicester and Swannington Railway in the early 1960s when my father obtained written permission from British Railways to walk along the line from Leicester to Desford. This included walking through the Glenfield Tunnel at a weekend when no trains were running, and visiting the signal box at Desford Junction. Later in the 1960s I moved away from Leicester and returned to NW Leicestershire in the 1990s where I became familiar with the Swannington end of the line. Since retiring I have become involved in two organisations involved in promoting the L&SR; the Leicestershire Industrial History Society and the Swannington Heritage Trust. They encouraged me to photograph and document what remains of the L&SR, and the result is this book.

This book shows what still exists of the railway today (2016), and shows some of the original features that can still be seen. Other publications (see further information section at the end) describe where you can find more information on the history of the line. Most of the sites shown can be visited in a day by car, but to see the Bagworth and Swannington Inclines involves walking along muddy paths. Also remember that part of the route is still an operational railway.

Many of these pictures were first shown at the 89th East Midlands Industrial Archaeology Conference in Swannington in October 2015.

I would like to thank my colleagues in the Leicestershire Industrial History Society and Swannington Heritage Trust for their help and advice in preparing this book. Special thanks are due to Paul Banbury for helping with the technical production of this book.

A note on the photographs

Most of the photographs in this book were taken in the period December 2014-February 2015. They are all taken from readily accessible public places, with the exception of the photographs of Glenfield Tunnel. It is only possible to visit the tunnel on special open days (see further information section at end of book for details). However bear in mind that changes occur and new developments might mean it is no longer possible to see a particular item or view.

A Brief History of the Leicester and Swannington Railway

Coal has been mined in the Swannington area of North West Leicestershire since the 13th C. The main market for this coal was Leicester, about 15 miles away, and it was transported there by pack horses along muddy tracks. Following the construction of the Erewash canal in 1779 and using the river Soar, coal from mines in Nottinghamshire and Derbyshire could be transported to Leicester a lot cheaper than the coal from NW Leicestershire, and so the Leicestershire mines were in danger of losing their main market. To remain competitive the Charnwood Forest canal and a series of horse drawn tramways to link the River Soar at Loughborough with the coalfield was opened in 1794. Disaster struck early on when the banks of Blackbrook reservoir that supplied water to the canal gave way and flooded the canal and destroyed its banks. The canal never recovered and gradually fell into disuse.

By the late 1820s, railways were starting to become a way of transporting coal, and local mine owners in the Swannington area thought that a railway to transport coal from their mines to Leicester would enable them to compete with coal from other parts of the country. William Stenson, the owner of coal mines near Swannington, and a Leicestershire business man and farmer, William Ellis, approached George Stephenson, the famous railway engineer,to see if he would construct such a railway.

George could see the potential of such a railway, and installed his son Robert as Engineer on the assumption that George would support him. George Stephenson established a home at Alton Grange near Ashby-de-la-Zouch during the period of construction of the line, and his stay was recently commemorated with a green plaque on the wall of the house.

Construction started in 1830 and the line opened in 1832. It is about 16 miles long, and was single track. Its main purpose was to carry coal from Swannington area to Leicester, but other coal mines along the route were connected to it. One of these to benefit was Whitwick colliery owned by William Stenson. Several rudimentary stations for passengers were established, but basically passengers stood at the side of the track and climbed up steps into open wagons.

In 1846 the Midland Railway (MR) bought out the L&SR and used the middle part of it (between what became Desford Junction and Mantle Lane Junction) as part of their Leicester to Burton upon Trent line. The MR made this line double track and so all of the original L&SR earthworks on this section were rebuilt to accommodate the extra track. The MR also abandoned the incline at Bagworth by constructing a new line on a reduced gradient that became known as the Thornton Deviation. The construction of the MR line from Leicester to Burton upon Trent had the effect of making the two ends of the original L&SR line into branch lines.

The Swannington branch from Mantle Lane Junction to the foot of the Swannington Incline closed in 1948. Coal mining in the Swannington and Coleorton areas had finished by the the 1870s, but the pumps at the former Calcutta colliery near the bottom of the incline needed to be kept operating to prevent deeper mines elsewhere from flooding. These pumps were operated by a steam engine and the coal for this engine was transported *down* the incline. So for the first part of its life coal was wound up the Swannington Incline, and for the second part it was wound down the incline!

The Leicester branch from Desford Junction to what became known as West Bridge Station soldiered on until the mid 1960s. The line closed to passengers in 1928, but freight trains (primarily coal) continued to the end.

The Route

This book follows the route of the L&SR from Swannington to Leicester, which is the reverse of the usual way of describing the line. I chose this direction because this was the direction the coal travelled, and the transport of coal was the reason for the construction the line in the first place.

The L&SR starts at the Northern end of Swannington village on Main Street. Near here at the foot of the Swannington Incline three tramways came together bringing coal in wagons from various mines in the area for despatch to Leicester. These wagons were wound to the top of the incline using a stationary steam powered winding engine. At the top a conventional train took the full wagons away. The route was through Coalville (then called Long Lane), across Ashby Road at Bardon, through Battleflat cutting to the top of the Bagworth Incline. Full wagons were lowered down the incline, and formed into another train at the bottom. The line then proceeded through Merrylees, Desford and Ratby before arriving at Glenfield. A mile long tunnel was constructed to avoid the line having to go over the hill in between Leicester and Glenfield. The terminus at Leicester was on the banks of the River Soar at what became known as West Bridge Station. Here was a short branch line that crossed the river and then the adjacent canal to Pingle Wharf on the far side of the canal.

The L&SR Today

The original route of the L&SR can be easily followed using the 1:25000 series OS maps and GoogleEarth. About half of the line (8 miles) is still an operating railway, albeit only freight and mainly stone from Bardon Hill Quarry. Of the remaining 8 miles or so, 4 miles is now either a footpath or footpath & cycle way. Glenfield Tunnel accounts for a further mile. The remaining 3 miles is on private land and so not accessible to the public However most of this can easily be seen on GoogleEarth. Only on either side of the Glenfield Tunnel has all trace of the L&SR been obliterated by housing developments.

Leicester and Swannington Railway Today

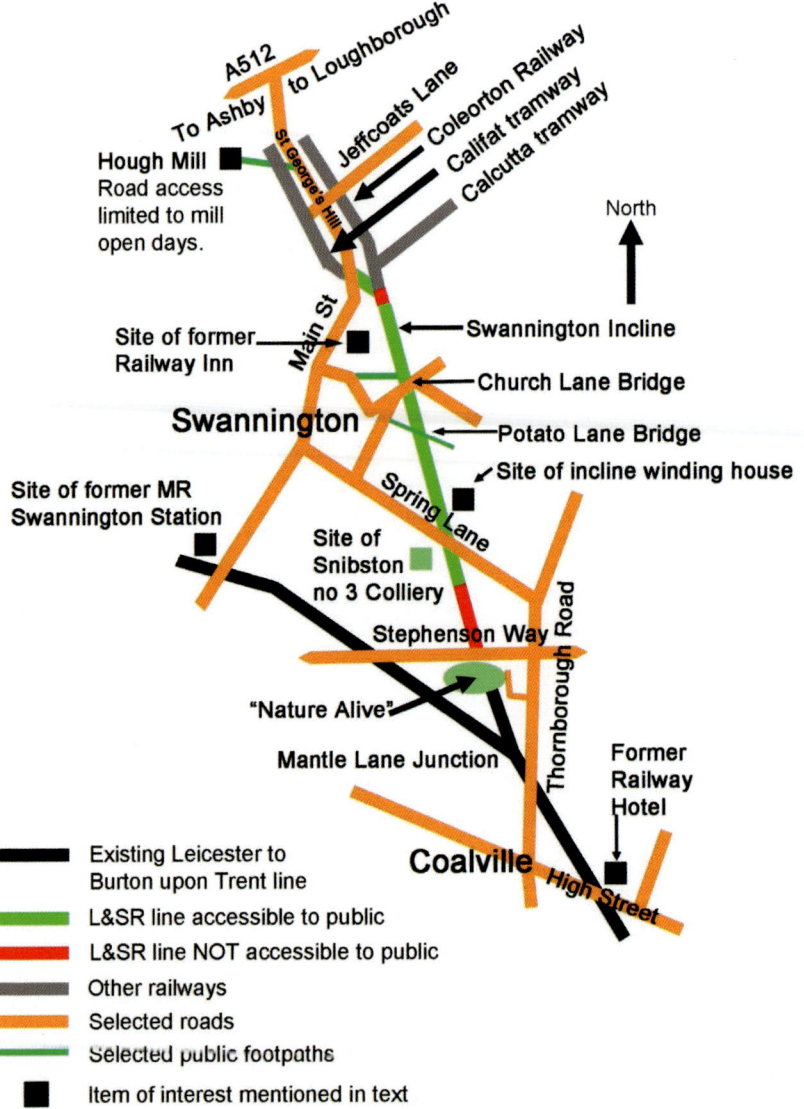

Swannington

The official start (or end) of L&SR is in Main Street, at the Northern end of Swannington village. It made an end-on connection with the Califat Tramway, which crossed the road here and continued up to the Califat Colliery. Traces of the tramway embankment can still be seen in places in the fields next to Main Street.

▲ Main Street Swannington, looking South. The L&SR terminated at the end of the track on the left, where it made an end on connection with the tramway that crossed the road and continued to Califat colliery. One of the tramways linking Swannington with the Charnwood Forest canal also started here, but all traces of it here have long since disappeared.

▼ Looking along the old track bed of L&SR from Main Street to the foot of Swannington Incline. The foot of the incline is now private land, and is where the Coleorton Railway and the tramway from Calcutta Colliery joined the L&SR. Please note that there is NO access to the Swannington Incline here.

Leicester and Swannington Railway Today

Swannington Incline

The Swannington Incline is about ½ mile long and rises at a gradient of 1:17. In 1832 this gradient was too steep for a conventional steam locomotive to haul full wagons up this incline. Instead full wagons of coal were hauled up by a rope powered by a stationary steam engine at the top. After the incline stopped operating in 1948, it became overgrown and used as a dumping ground. The Swannington Heritage Trust acquired it in 1984 and set about clearing the site. They also made the route a permissive path so enabling the public to see the incline once more. However, note that there is no public access at the bottom of the incline; you have to either return to the top or use one of the footpaths and roads that cross it.

► Cattle Arch Bridge, which allows cattle to pass under the incline. A new bridge was built in 1986 to replace the original one that had become badly damaged by mining subsidence and was subsequently demolished.

▼ To help reduce the gradient of the incline, the lower part is built on an embankment, while the upper part (opposite page bottom) is in a cutting.

Leicester and Swannington Railway Today

▲ Church Lane Bridge. After the closure of the incline in 1948, this part was used as rubbish dump The Swannington Heritage Trust removed all the accumulated rubbish in 1990s and arranged for the bridge to be rebuilt.

▼ Looking up the incline from Church Lane bridge. This part of the incline is in a cutting to help reduce the gradient.

Leicester and Swannington Railway Today

Top of the Swannington Incline

▲ Looking down the incline from the top, with the brick built Church Lane Bridge visible in the distance. The wooden Potato Lane Bridge carrying a footpath is also just visible above Church Lane Bridge.

▼ The stationary engine winding house was located near the top of the incline. The track passed between the two prominent gate posts on the left and over the two marked squares on the left. The furthest away of these held the winding drum, while the nearer was a coal drop. The coal was used to fire the boiler which produced the steam to drive the stationary winding engine (see page 10).

◀ This engine at the top of the incline is nothing to do with the L&SR!. It is from Calcutta pumping station and was used to lift out the pump rods for servicing. It was donated to the Swannington Heritage Trust by the NCB when the mine finally stopped pumping in 1986.

▲ Outline of boiler house and chimney.

▼ Model of the top of Swannington Incline made by the late LIHS member Dennis Hill and now on display at Hough mill, Swannington. The brick buildings on the right contained the boiler and winding engine and the houses on the left were where the incline operators lived.

Leicester and Swannington Railway Today

When the line was built in 1832, the incline out of Swannington was too steep for conventional steam railway engines to operate on it and so a stationary steam engine was installed to wind full wagons up the incline, and control the speed of empty ones going downhill. The 1833 stationary steam winding engine that was used to haul wagons up the Swannington Incline was preserved when the incline closed in 1948 and is now on display in National Railway Museum, York.

Leicester and Swannington Railway Today

Swannington Incline

During the reclaiming of the incline, the Swannington Heritage Trust discovered various items associated with its operation.

◄ One of the dolly rollers that was located between the rails on the incline to guide the haulage rope.

▼ Ratchet that was part of the control mechanism for starting and stopping the main winding drum.

▼ A section of the original L&SR fish bellied rail.

▼ A hook used to connect wagons to the haulage rope.

▲ Hough Mill, where items shown on this page can be seen. See Swannington Heritage Trust website for opening times.

11

Top of Swannington Incline

▲ Looking away from the site of the winding engine towards Spring Lane and Coalville. This was where passengers from Swannington would have boarded the trains to Leicester. However, first they would have had to book their tickets at the Railway Inn in the middle of Swannington village, over half a mile away. After the takeover of the L&SR by the Midland Railway and the completion of the line to Burton upon Trent, this section was closed to passenger traffic, and a new station (complete with booking office!) Was constructed on Hough Hill.

◄ Level crossing gatepost at Spring Lane.

▼ Track bed continues on the other side of Spring Lane, next to the site of Snibston No 3 Colliery, which is now a picnic site.

Site of Snibston No 3

"Nature Alive", Coalville

"Nature Alive" is a nature reserve in Coalville; the entrance is between the Aldi supermarket and Archie Moss Garage on Thornborough Road. The L&SR crossed this site on an embankment. The bridge below is probably a Stephenson original.

Leicester and Swannington Railway Today

At the edge of "Nature Alive" the Swannington Branch joins the current Leicester to Burton upon Trent line at what became known as Mantle Lane Junction. The original L&SR line is to the right of the buffer stop (above) and continues along the left hand side in the picture below (taken looking in the opposite direction to the one above).

BE AWARE THAT SOME OF THESE LINES ARE STILL USED BY TRAINS TODAY

Coalville

The original single track L&SR section of line from Mantle Lane Junction to Desford Junction was rebuilt by the Midland Railway as double track. As a result virtually all of the original L&SR earthworks and infrastructure were destroyed, However there are still some interesting historical items to see on this section.

▲ When the L&SR was constructed, Coalville was only a very small village known as Long Lane. The former Railway Hotel (now a children's nursery) is next to the level crossing on High Street and is where tickets for the railway were sold prior to the construction of the station on the opposite side of the road.

▼ Bardon Hill signal box, an original Midland Railway style signal box, at the level crossing near Bardon Quarry Sidings. Stone from Bardon Quarry is now the main source of traffic on the Leicester to Burton upon Trent line following the closure of the coal mines in this area.

Battleflat Cutting

▲ This wharf was built in 1894 and was the terminus of the Cliffe Hill Railway. This railway was a two foot gauge line built to carry granite from the quarries to the main line. The track bed of the first part of this line can still be seen and is a public footpath. The wharf can be seen from the bridge over the main Leicester to Burton upon Trent line on the road from Bardon Industrial Estate to Ellistown.

▼ The route through Battleflat Cutting has been affected by mining subsidence, as this photograph taken from one of the footpaths that crosses the line shows. The bridge in the distance is next to the wharf shown above.

Leicester and Swannington Railway Today

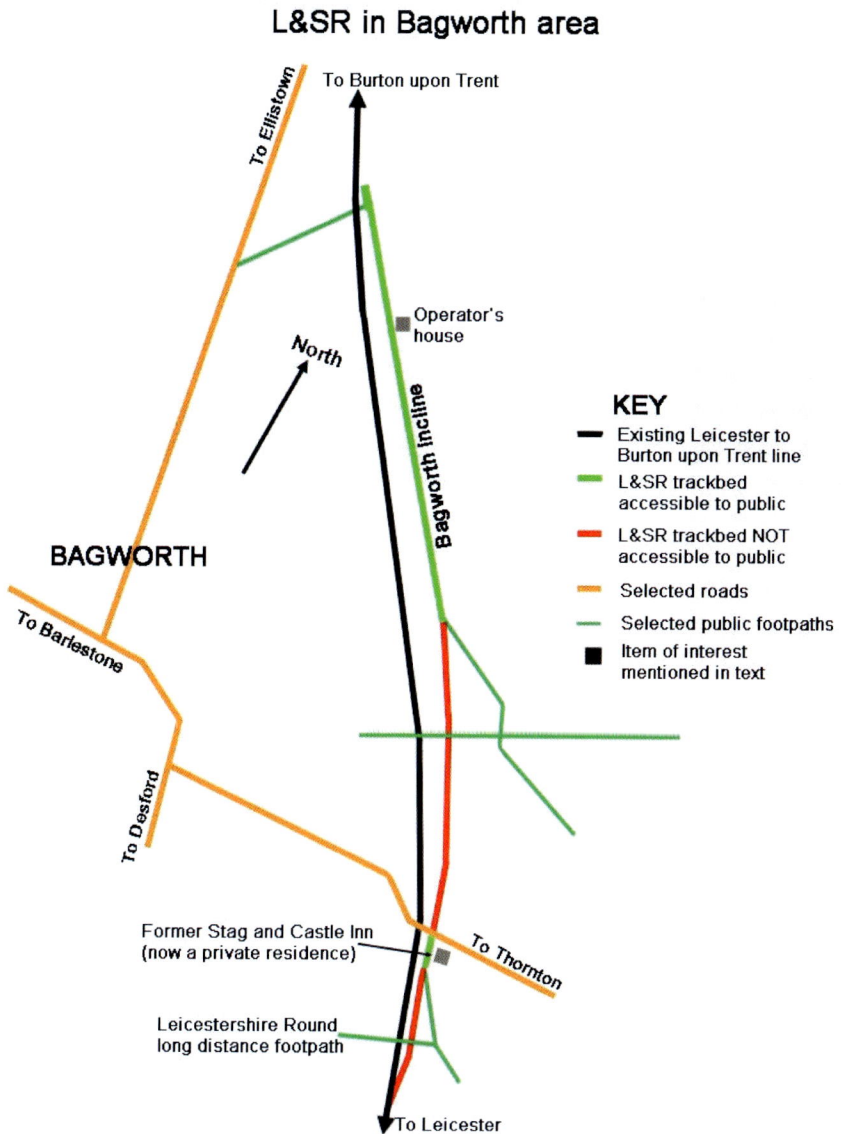

Leicester and Swannington Railway Today

Bagworth Incline

This was a down hill incline for coal traffic heading towards Leicester and was a self acting one; the weight of the full coal wagons descending the incline was sufficient to haul the same number of empty wagons up the incline. The Midland Railway abandoned the Bagworth Incline when it built what became known as the Thornton Deviation on the Leicester to Burton upon Trent line. The incline is now a public footpath.

▲ Top of the incline, where the horizontal pulley wheel for the rope would be located in the ground. No trace of the wheel now remains.

▼ The steepness of the incline can be appreciated in this view looking down the incline.

Leicester and Swannington Railway Today

Operator's House, Bagworth Incline

The incline operator's house was given Grade II listed status in the 1980s as it was the last remaining original Stephenson built L&SR building. Sadly the listing has not prevented it falling into disrepair and today it is little more than a pile of bricks. It can be found near the top of the incline next to the footpath hidden in some trees and undergrowth.

Bagworth Incline

▲ The bottom of the Bagworth Incline looking back towards the top. The Thornton Deviation runs along the far side of the field on the left behind the trees. At the bottom of the incline the public footpath leaves the route of the L&SR.

▼From the bottom of the incline, the L&SR ran across these fields, where the original Bagworth Station was located. No trace of this now remains.

Former Stag and Castle Inn

The Stag and Castle was an inn on the Bagworth to Thornton road and was a stopping place on the L&SR. It closed as a stopping point in 1841. The former inn is now a private residence.

The original L&SR crossed the Bagworth - Thornton road through the gate on the right and then up the driveway on the left and past the former Stag and Castle Inn (below). It was at this crossing that a train hauled by *Samson* collided with a horse and cart, and as a result the L&SR decided to equip all its locomotives with steam whistles to act as a warning to other traffic. The bridge in the background carries the current Leicester to Burton upon Trent line on the Thornton Deviation.

Leicester and Swannington Railway Today

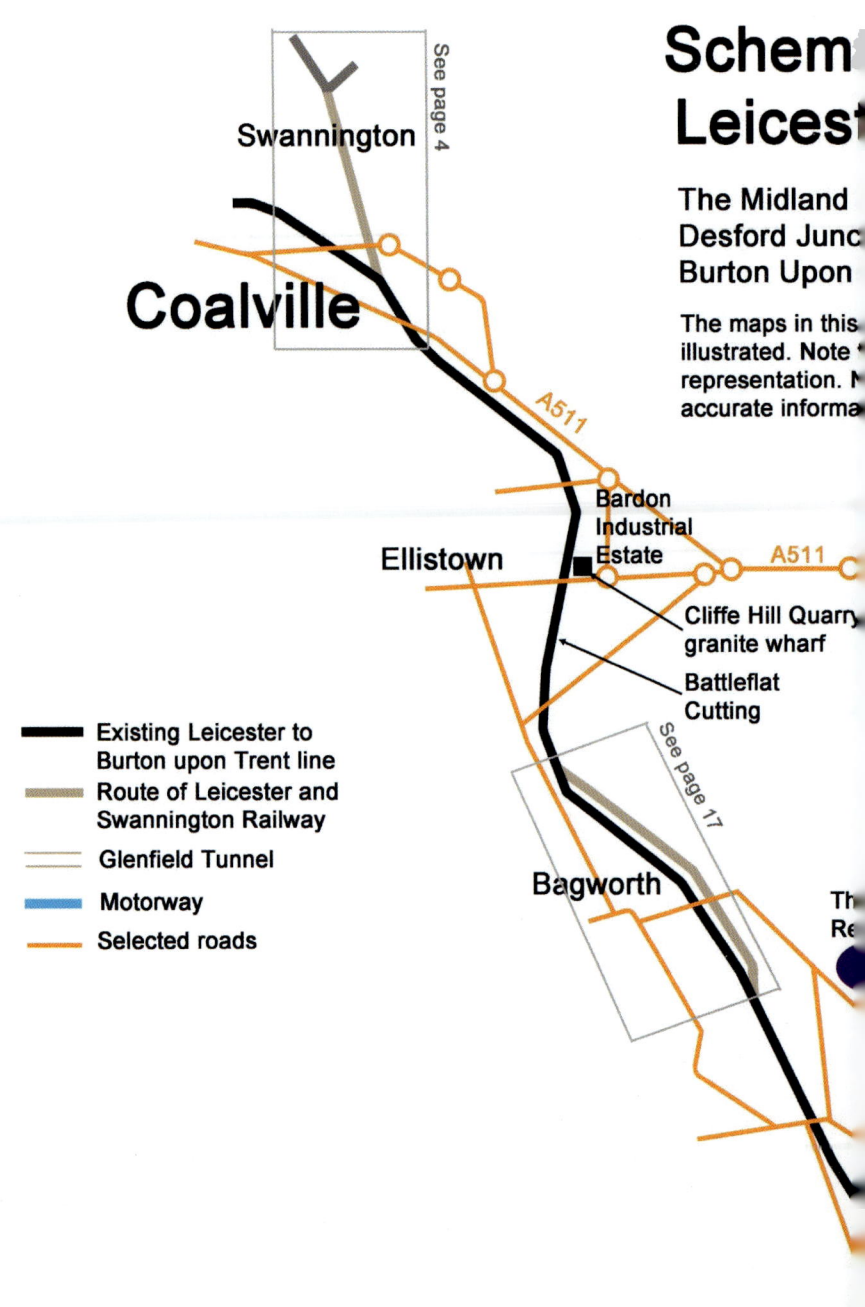

Leicester and Swannington Railway Today

ic map showing route of the
r and Swannington Railway

lway incorporated the middle section of the L&SR from
to Mantle Lane Junction (Coalville) into their Leicester to
nt railway. This railway is still in use today.

k are intended to help the reader identify where to find the various sites
the maps are to different scales, and are not intended to be an accurate
ll roads, tracks and footpaths are shown. Readers requiring more
are recommended to use a relevant OS map.

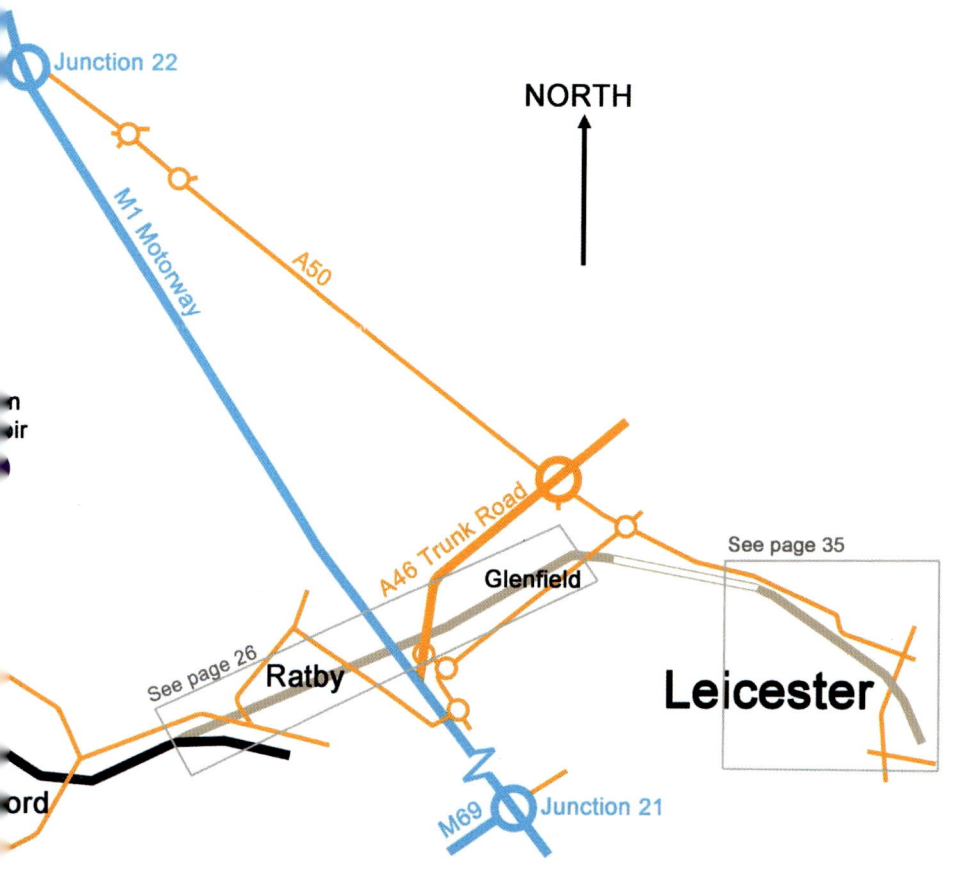

L&SR meets Leicestershire Round footpath

From the former Stag and Castle Inn, the original track bed of the L&SR is now a farm track (above). This is not a public footpath but there is one running parallel in the field on the left.

This track and footpath meet the Leicestershire Round long distance footpath, which then crosses the existing Leicester to Burton upon Trent line which is on the right.

The steps up to today's railway (left) are almost certainly made out of the original L&SR stone sleepers (below).

Leicester and Swannington Railway Today

About ½ mile further South along the existing Leicester to Burton upon Trent line another footpath crosses the line, and once again the steps up to the line are almost certainly made from former L&SR stone sleepers.

In some of these can be seen the holes where wooden pegs were inserted. The chairs that held the rails in place were then fixed to these wooden pegs using metal spikes.

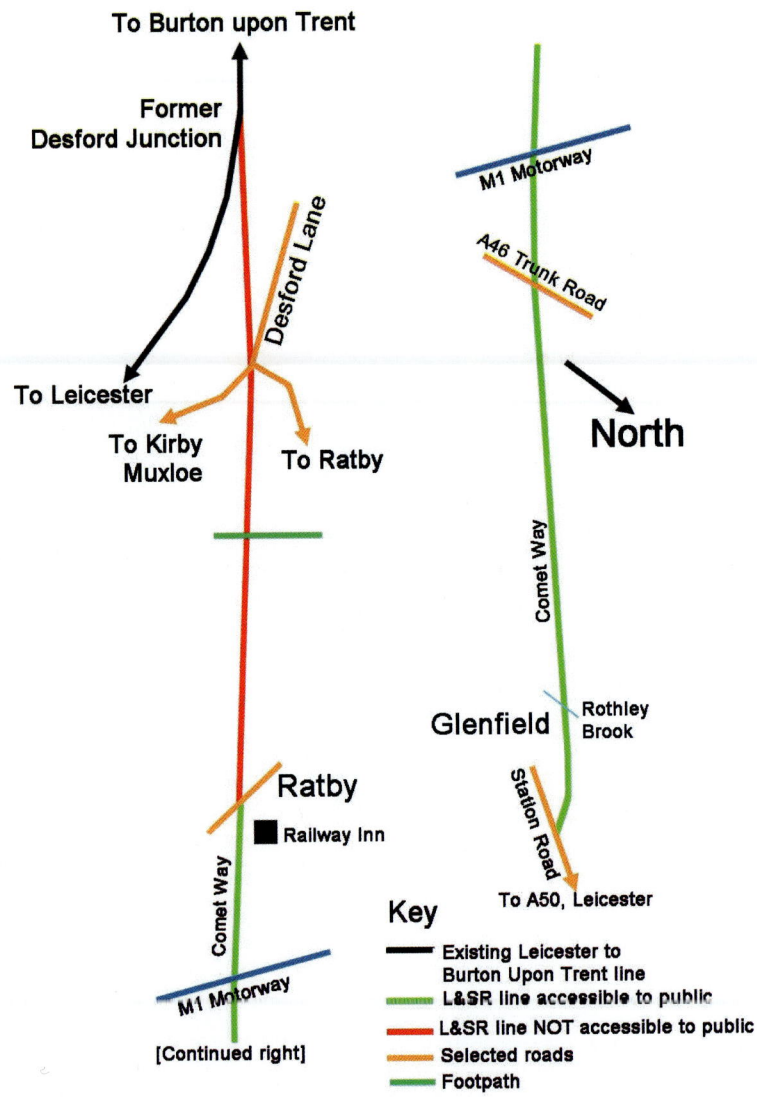

Ratby

The former Desford Junction is where the Midland Railway from Leicester to Burton upon Trent joined the original L&SR, making the original L&SR to Leicester a branch line. There is no public access to the site of Desford Junction, and the track bed as far as Ratby is across private land with no public access apart from one footpath that crosses it. However the route can easily be followed on the 1:25000 OS map and GoogleEarth.

◀ Site of Ratby station built at a later date by the Midland Railway, which is now an industrial unit. There was a level crossing across this road here.

The Railway Inn, is next to the site of the original L&SR station and was where passengers booked and purchased their tickets. A plaque on the wall commemorates this role.

Leicester and Swannington Railway Today

By the side of the Railway Inn is the start of Comet Way, a footpath and cycle way that follows the original L&SR track bed to Glenfield, two miles away. *Comet* was the name of one of the original L&SR steam locomotives.

There is a buffer stop containing a plaque giving details of the L&SR. On the ground in front of it is a section of fish bellied rail resting in chairs fixed to two stone sleepers.

Leicester and Swannington Railway Today

Glenfield

The village of Glenfield is proud of its association with the L&SR to the extent that the village sign in the centre of the village depicts a train leaving the Glenfield Tunnel.

▼ Comet Way as it enters Glenfield. If you look carefully in the hedges at the side as you walk or cycle along, you can see remains of railway old gate and fence posts.

▼ Bridge over Rothley Brook. There is a popular story that when the first train passed through Glenfield Tunnel on the opening day, its chimney fouled the tunnel roof and covered all the passengers, who were seated in open trucks, with soot and cinders! After emerging from the tunnel, the train then stopped here so that the passengers could clean themselves up in the stream.

Leicester and Swannington Railway Today

▲ The mile post and these buffer stop are the only remaining evidence that that was ever a railway here.

▲ Comet Way ends on Station Road, Glenfield, next to yet another Railway Inn where L&SR tickets were originally sold. The mile post on the left indicates 3 miles from West Bridge Station.

▼ Opposite the end of Comet Way was the site of Glenfield Station, which has been completely obliterated by a housing development called, appropriately enough, Stephenson Court, and no trace of the station remains. The railway crossed Station Road roughly where the mini roundabout is located.

Glenfield Tunnel

Glenfield Tunnel is the largest and most significant remaining part of the original L&SR. It took two years to construct and required an estimated five million bricks to line it. It is just over a mile long and at the time it was the longest steam railway tunnel in the world.

After the closure of the West Bridge branch in the 1960s, Leicester City Council acquired the tunnel. In the 2000s the Council strengthened parts of the tunnel, particularly around the air shafts. In 2013 the Leicester Industrial History Society (LIHS) were granted permission to take visitors into the tunnel. Details of future open days can be found in the further information section at the end of this book.

Please note that the Western tunnel entrance (ie Glenfield end) is on Leicester City Council ground and is only accessible and visible on open days. The Eastern portal at the Leicester end of the tunnel has been bricked up, covered over and a housing estate built over it, and so is no longer accessible or visible.

Leicester and Swannington Railway Today

▲ A view inside the tunnel. LIHS are allowed to take visitors about 400 metres inside the tunnel. The blue hose (since removed) on the left wall is left over from earlier stabilisation work. The temperature inside the tunnel is fairly constant throughout the year at about 12°C.

▼ One of the reinforcing rings installed by the council to strengthen the tunnel and prevent subsidence damage to properties above.

▼Refuges were built into the side of the tunnel as a place where workmen working inside could stand when a train passed through.

Glenfield Tunnel was the longest railway tunnel in the world when it was constructed. The only comparable tunnels of a similar length had been constructed for canals, and so similar design and construction techniques were employed. Hence the tunnel is dead straight and level.

Shafts like this one were sunk at intervals from the surface along the projected line of the tunnel. When they reached the required depth, they tunnelled outwards in both directions until they met similar excavations from neighbouring shafts.

After the tunnel was completed these construction shafts, together with some specially constructed smaller shafts, became ventilation shafts to help remove the steam and smoke from passing trains. In total 13 shafts were constructed.

Leicester and Swannington Railway Today

◄ Some of the ventilation shafts are now in private gardens, whereas others are by the side of public roads. This one is probably the easiest one to find. It is located at the corner of New Parks Way and Kemp Road, close to the roundabout on Groby Road by Glenfield Hospital.

▼ Copeland Avenue, Leicester. The Eastern portal (ie Leicester end) of Glenfield Tunnel is now buried below this road and housing estate.

Leicester and Swannington Railway Today

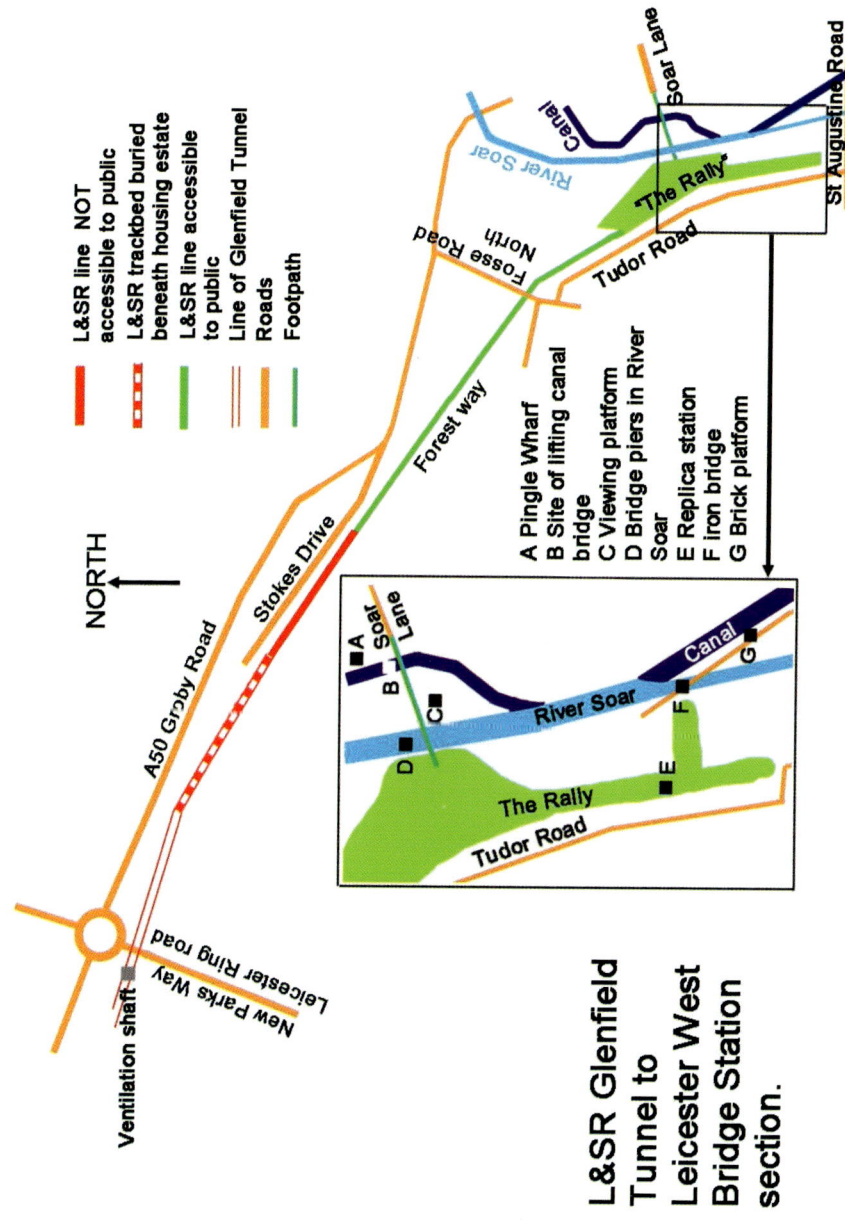

Leicester

◄ A housing estate and allotments have been built over the first part of the track bed of the L&SR from Glenfield Tunnel. However George Stephenson is remembered by one of the estate roads being named after the village near Newcastle upon Tyne where he was born. Other examples of roads being named after people associated with the L&SR exist.

▼ After the housing estate the former track bed has become the Forest Way footpath and cycle way.

▲ Forest Way crosses over Fosse Road North on a new footbridge resting on the former railway bridge parapets. Originally there was a level crossing here but it was replaced by a bridge by the Midland Railway in the 1890s.

"The Rally", Leicester

The Leicester terminus of the L&SR was on the banks of the River Soar, and later became known as West Bridge Station to differentiate from other railway stations that were subsequently built in Leicester. Most of the former station site has been converted into a park called The Rally. The above picture shows Forest Way entering the park. The houses on the left are on Tudor Road, and the backs of these houses are a prominent feature of many photographs of West Bridge Station when it was in use.

There is a viewing mound on the other side of the river from The Rally that gives a good view of the former West Bridge Station area.

Leicester and Swannington Railway Today

The original L&SR station was on an island between the canal and River Soar. The L&SR crossed the River Soar on the iron bridge (shown above and left), and terminated at the side of the canal (roughly where the people on the canal towpath are in above photograph). A 1895 map of the area shows a brick platform as part of the station on the banks of the canal. Further research is required to determine whether the current wall (below) is part of the original L&SR station. Part of this wall can also be seen on the left in the top photograph.

Leicester and Swannington Railway Today

The original L&SR station was built next to the canal. In the 1890s the Midland Railway built a new station on the opposite side of the site. This station was demolished after the line closed, but a short replica station platform and signal has been erected on the site of the former Midland Railway station.

River Soar, Leicester

The L&SR constructed a short branch line from West Bridge Station across the River Soar to Pingle Wharf on the the canal on the far side. All that remain are the bridge pillars standing in the river.

Canal, Leicester

After crossing the River Soar, the branch line also had to cross the canal since Pingle's Wharf was on the far side. A lifting bridge was used to allow canal traffic to pass under the branch.

▲ The lifting bridge was situated next to this bridge, which carries Soar Lane across the canal.

▼ The lifting bridge was saved and up until July 2015 was on display outside the Snibston Discovery Museum in Coalville. With the closure of that museum its fate is unclear.

Leicester and Swannington Railway Today

If you look closely in the undergrowth by the side of the road bridge over the canal you can see the remains of some old rails. These are not original L&SR ones.

Leicester and Swannington Railway Today

1966 Photographs

▲ West Bridge station buildings.

▲ Glenfield tunnel portal and station.

▶ Ratby Station

▼ Desford Junction looking North East. The L&SR line to West Bridge is to the left of the signal box, while the train is on the ex MR Leicester to Burton upon Trent line.

43

Further information

General Histories

The Leicester & Swannington Railway by CR Clinker (Avon Anglia Publication, 1977)

Leicestershire Industrial History Society (LIHS).

LIHS has produced a number of publications (available for sale via their website) on the L&SR including:

The Leicester and Swannington railway in a nutshell (28 pages). This is a layperson's guide to one of the world's first steam railways.

Glenfield Tunnel (24 pages). The story of a most historic hole in the ground.

Leicester & Swannington Update 2010: compendium (e book 600 pages) Contains a wealth of information on the L&SR including many photographs, maps and drawings. It is an Adobe PDF document for viewing on a computer.

LIHS also organise visits into Glenfield Tunnel. The tunnel is usually open ten days per year (six in July during the Archaeology fortnight, and four in September) and there are 4 tours per day. Each tour is limited to 25 people. Advanced booking is essential. Details of dates and how to apply will appear on the LIHS website about 2 months beforehand. Tours for societies or other groups can also usually be arranged.

Website: www.lihs.org.uk

Swannington Heritage Trust (SHT)

SHT own and maintain the Swannington Incline and other historic sites in the village. They have produced the following booklets relating to the L&SR:

Notes on the Leicester and Swannington Railway by Clement E Stretton. A transcript of a lecture given in 1891.

Swannington: One-Time Railway Centre by Charles E Lee. A reprint of an 1939 article in *The Railway magazine*.

The Trust's website (www.swannington-heritage.co.uk) also gives more information on the incline, and the opening times of Hough mill where the artefacts shown on page 11 and the model shown on page 9 can be seen.